1ST GRADE UNITED STATES HISTORY:

EARLY AMERICAN SETTLERS

Native Americans were grouped into tribes or nations. These groupings were generally based on peoples that shared the same culture, language, religion, customs, and politics.

The Apache
traditionally lived in
the Southern Great
Plains including
Texas, Arizona,
New Mexico,
and Oklahoma.

The Apache used
bows and arrows
to hunt. Bow strings
were made from
animal tendons.

Cherokee Indians are a tribe of American Indian people who were moved from the Great Lakes region to the Appalachian Mountains.

The Cherokee Indians are largest tribe in the United States. The Cherokee lived off a combination of farming, hunting, and gathering.

The Blackfoot lived in teepees made from bison hides and wooden poles. The Blackfoot enjoyed decorating their clothing and their teepees.

The main food for the Blackfoot came from the bison. The Blackfoot wore clothing made from deerskin.

The Cheyenne Indians were far-ranging people, especially once they acquired horses. A Cheyenne woman built her family's house.